A GUIDE

GU00984587

THE PALACE OF

NESTOR,

MYCENAEAN SITES IN ITS ENVIRONS
AND
THE CHORA MUSEUM

American School of Classical Studies at Athens
Princeton, NJ

2001

Figure 1. Sketch map of western Messenia

FOREWORD[1]

The purpose of this booklet is to provide the visitor to western Messenia (Fig. 1) with a compact guide to the Palace of Nestor, excavated by Carl W. Blegen and Marion Rawson between 1939 and 1971, and to principal excavated Mycenaean sites nearby.[2] The excavators' pamphlet, "A Guide to the Palace of Nestor," is here reprinted with revisions and short footnotes to clarify the text and to bring it up to date. Color illustrations substitute, where possible, for the original black-and-whites. In addition to these changes, we have added a short introduction to excavated monuments in the vicinity of the Palace of Nestor, and a discussion of the economy, society, and politics of the

Pylos kingdom during Late Helladic IIIB (ca. 1300–1200 B.C.). The decipherment of the many documents found in the remnants of the palace has provided a vivid picture of life in Mycenaean times. At the same time archaeologists have been encouraged to seek out the many settlements controlled by the palace and mentioned by name in its records. The Palace of Nestor did not stand alone on its citadel on the ridge of Englianos. The visitor to Pylos can today catch a glimpse of the entire ancient landscape that surrounded it.

We have also added a section on the Chora Museum, which contains finds from the palace and other sites in the area.

(JLD and CWS)

HISTORY OF THE EXCAVATIONS AT THE PALACE OF NESTOR

In 1912 and 1926 Dr. Konstantine Kourouniotis excavated two tholos ("beehive") tombs in the region north of the Bay of Navarino.[3] Both had been plundered in ancient times, but each yielded interesting overlooked objects. One contained three handsome jars decorated in the "palace style," the other a collection of Early Mycenaean and Middle Helladic pots.[4] In the general neighborhood Kourouniotis observed surface indications of several further tombs of the same type.

A joint Hellenic-American expedition was formed, with Kourouniotis representing the Greek Archaeological Service and Carl W. Blegen the University of Cincinnati. The purpose of the undertaking was to explore western Messenia with special reference to Mycenaean sites and cemeteries. In 1938 the two colleagues made a brief survey of the region. They believed that the tholos tombs were royal sepulchers, and they drew the conclusion that in a region where there are many such tombs there must be a palace in which the kings lived before they died and were buried.[5]

In 1939 more systematic explorations of the district to the east and north of the Bay of Navarino were carried out with the help of local residents, especially Charalambos Christophilopoulos of Koryphasion, who generously offered their information and guidance to places where ancient remains were known to exist. In the course of ten days, some seven or eight sites were discovered, all of which, on the evidence of the pottery lying on the ground, seemed to go back to the Mycenaean period. The most dominating position of all was on a hill called Epano Englianos, which commands a magnificent view: the Bay of Navarino to the south, the range of Mount Aigaleon toward the north and northeast, a wide expanse of rugged hills to the east, and more hills and the sea to the west. Two masses of hard concrete-like debris projected from the ground in the olive grove that occupied the hill.

Trial excavations were begun on April 4, 1939, and on the very first day stone walls, fragments of frescoes, stucco floors, five inscribed tablets, and Mycenaean pottery were brought to light. It became clear that a palace did exist here, just as the presence of important tombs had suggested. Explorations in the following weeks revealed that the building was of considerable extent, comparable to those already known at Tiryns, Mycenae, and Thebes.[6] More than six hundred tablets and fragments of tablets bearing inscriptions in the Linear B script were recovered during that first season.[7] Plans for beginning a systematic excavation the following year could not be realized because of the outbreak of World War II, and it was only in 1952 that work could be resumed.

Dr. Kourouniotis died in 1945, and Professor Spyridon Marinatos was designated by the Archaeological Council as his successor. Rather than conducting operations jointly, he preferred to concentrate his attention on the exploration of other settlement sites, tholos tombs, and chamber tombs in a wider neighborhood, while the Cincinnati Expedition devoted its chief efforts to the clearing of the palace and the investigation of its more immediate vicinity.

Through fifteen annual seasons from 1952 to 1966 the Palace of Nestor was gradually uncovered, while all areas on and just below the acropolis were widely explored. Financial support for the undertaking was provided by Professor and Mrs. William T. Semple until 1962, and subsequently by the Classics Fund of the University of Cincinnati, a gift of Louise Taft Semple in memory of her father, Charles Phelps Taft.

In the winter of 1960–1961 the Greek Archaeological Service erected a protective metal roof over the entire central building of the palace. It has thus been possible to leave most of the floors, hearths, and other elements uncovered and open to view by visitors whatever the season and weather.

(CWB and MR, JLD and CWS)

Blegen, Rawson, and their colleagues published their discoveries at the Palace of Nestor in a series of large, well-illustrated books: *The Palace of Nestor at Pylos in Western Messenia.*[8] The third volume appeared in 1973, after Blegen's death. A fourth and final volume, now in preparation, will contain the definitive edition of the Linear B tablets found in the palace.

Archaeology has changed considerably since the completion of excavations at the Palace of Nestor. Modern approaches and techniques allow new information to be extracted from material gathered in the past. During the 1990s, members of several archaeological teams have reexamined the work of Blegen and Rawson. Architects from the University of Minnesota have prepared a complete stone-by-stone plan of the site (http://marwp.cla.umn.edu/index.html). One goal of the Pylos Regional Archaeological Project has been to determine accurately the size of the town that surrounded the palace (http://classics.lsa.umich.edu/PRAP.html). And, since 1996, the University of Cincinnati and the Institute of Aegean Prehistory have supported the publication and republication of finds stored in the Chora Museum.

(JLD and CWS)

Figure 2. The Englianos hill with the palace from the northeast

THE SITE

The hill of Epano Englianos is situated close beside and to the west of the highway, some 4 km (2.4 miles) south of Chora and 17 km (10.2 miles) north of Pylos. The elevation (ca. 150 m, or 492 feet, above sea level), which has a maximum length of about 170 m (558 feet) from southwest to northeast and a width not exceeding 90 m (295 feet), rises abruptly on all sides in a steep, almost precipitous bank, some 4 to 7 m (13 to 23 feet) high. It is only toward the easternmost angle that a relatively narrow terrace descends somewhat lower, but even there access to the plateau could be gained only by a rough scramble up the bank until in 1952 the excavators cut an entrance way ascending through the steep slope.

The height had first been occupied by a settlement of the Middle Bronze Age,[9] but before the palace was erected the summit of the hill was apparently cut down and leveled out. From this time on—about the beginning of the 13th century B.C.—this end of the hill seems to have been reserved for the administrative center and related buildings.

On the slopes and terraces below to the northwest, southwest, and southeast Blegen excavated small parts of a lower town where the ordinary people lived. Investigations by the Pylos Regional Archaeological Project have since shown that the settlement also continued to the northeast; in fact, it was a substantial Mycenaean town that extended for hundreds of meters along the Englianos Ridge, and covered about 20 hectares (1 hectare = 10,000 square m, or 2.47 acres). Only a short distance to the northeast and southwest of the acropolis are tholos ("beehive") tombs, the burial places of royalty and the elite, and, on a ridge descending toward the west, chamber tombs of ordinary people have been found.

The palace occupies only a little more than the southwestern half of the hill (Fig. 2), and the northeastern half seems to have been left open without large buildings, as at Tiryns. No contemporary fortification wall has been securely identified at Epano Englianos, although there was an Early Mycenaean circuit wall with a gateway at the northeast end of the site (see below, page 37).[10] Several hundred meters west of the main palatial buildings, outside the fence that surrounds the site, subsurface geophysical prospection by the Pylos Regional Archaeological Project has located the foundations of a wall several meters thick that might also have defended the settlement at one stage in its history.

THE PALACE

The palace is a complex consisting of various buildings. The central unit, more than 50 m long and 32 m wide (ca. 163 × 104 feet), evidently housed the administrative offices of the Pylos kingdom, storage facilities, and residential quarters. It is centered on the throne room (6), a large rectangular room with a central hearth (see plan, inside back cover). This was the principal hall of state, where the king met with elite members of society and carried out rituals. To the southwest another similar building, smaller than the central one but still of considerable size, may perhaps be the earliest element of the complex, so far as the date of its construction is concerned; but both were certainly occupied down through the 13th century until the whole establishment was destroyed in a great fire not far from 1200 B.C. This building too contained residential and storage facilities and formal apartments of state, and like the Main Building, it seems to have had a separate wine storehouse (called by Blegen and Rawson the Wine Magazine) lying to the north, more-or-less behind it. There was also toward the northeast a fairly large separate building that served as the palace workshop, where spare parts for chariots seem to have been kept and repairs of metal and leather goods were carried out. To the northwest, between this building and the Wine Magazine and behind the central wing, there were also some smaller buildings. Blegen and Rawson thought they were perhaps for the accommodation of servants and slaves, but their purpose remains uncertain.

ARCHITECTURE

Wood was freely used in all parts of the construction of the palace, even the stone walls being erected within a massive framework of large horizontal and vertical timbers.

Figure 3. Main Building from the southeast

Columns, door-casings, wainscoting, ceilings, and roofs were also constructed mainly of wood, and this abundance of combustible material accounts for the devastating effect of the fire that destroyed the palace. The exterior walls on all sides were built with an outer facing of fine squared blocks of limestone (poros) laid in neat rows with the outside facing smoothed off, while rubble was used for the inner facing. The interior walls were constructed mainly of rubble, though large stones and squared blocks were often used there too. The faces of the interior walls were coated with plaster, and those in all important rooms were decorated with frescoes.

The Main and Southwestern buildings were two-storied, each having stairways leading to the upper floor. The latter evidently had walls built of rude brick laid in the usual framework of wooden beams. The roof was probably formed by flat terraces, perhaps in two or more levels. The roof over the throne room (6) was certainly higher than that on each side.

MAIN BUILDING

The principal entrance to the main building of the palace was on the southeastern side, approached across a broad open stucco-paved court (Fig. 3). A gateway separated two shaded porches (propylon 1 and 2 on the plan), each with a single column to support the roof. The stone bases of the columns have survived, with remains of the stucco ring that decorated the lower end of the wooden shaft. The columns were fluted with sixty-four flutings, as shown by the impressions left in the stucco ring. On entering the outer porch (1) one encountered a sentry stand at the left of the doorway; as well as the main entrance, the sentry may have guarded a door that led into the archives complex (7 and 8), a suite of two small rooms beside the gateway.[11] Here were found nearly one thousand clay tablets and fragments, inscribed in the Linear B script. Michael Ventris, in June 1952, succeeded in finding the key to the Linear B script, which proved to represent an early stage of Greek. The documents,

Figure 4. Linear B tablets

which can now in considerable part be read, have turned out to be economic and administrative records of the Pylos kingdom (Fig. 4).

Proceeding through the gateway one entered an interior courtyard (3), open to the sky, beyond which rose the portico (4) of the state apartments, with two columns in its façade between projecting side walls (Fig. 5). At the left was another suite of two chambers, apparently a pantry (9) and a waiting room (10), into which visitors could be ushered to await their turn to be introduced into the royal presence. The waiting room (10) was provided with a bench, coated with stucco, which bore painted patterns; here the guests could sit until summoned. In the corner was a clay stand, also stuccoed and painted, which contained two large jars, perhaps for wine. The connecting room (9) was a pantry with wooden shelves on which stood hundreds of wine cups. The guests thus seem to have been offered refresh-

Figure 5. Palace courtyard

ments while they waited. The cups now lie on the floor, warped, distorted, and vitrified by the heat as they fell when the shelves that held them were consumed by the fire that destroyed the palace.

When the time came, one proceeded through the portico (4) with its two columns, only the stone bases of which survive. The walls seem to have been rather elaborately decorated with wooden wainscoting and panels. To the right, beside the doorway, is the stand for another sentry or attendant. Through the doorway one reached a vestibule (5) which, like the portico, had a painted stucco floor and gaily frescoed walls. Straight ahead, guarded by yet another sentry, was still another doorway through which one entered the principal hall of state, the throne room (6).

In the center is a great ceremonial hearth, made of clay coated with stucco and rising some 20 cm (8 inches) above the floor (Fig. 6). It was framed by four nearly symmetri-

Figure 6. Ceremonial hearth, throne room

cally spaced wooden columns, which rested on stone bases and supported a surrounding balcony and a high clerestory or lantern. The latter served perhaps for air and light, and smoke from the hearth could escape through a chimney made of two sections of terracotta pipe that were carried through the roof. The royal throne was nearly centered against the right-hand wall, facing the hearth; all that remains is the cutting made for it in the stuccoed floor. The throne itself was made of perishable material, probably wood, no doubt decorated with ivory or other inlaid work.

This spacious hall, 12.90 m long and 11.20 m wide (42.3 × 36.8 feet), was bright with multicolored painted decoration. The floor was laid out in squares (Fig. 7), each bearing linear patterns in red, yellow, blue, white and black, and perhaps other colors. Only in front of the throne was there a somewhat realistic representation, of a huge octopus.

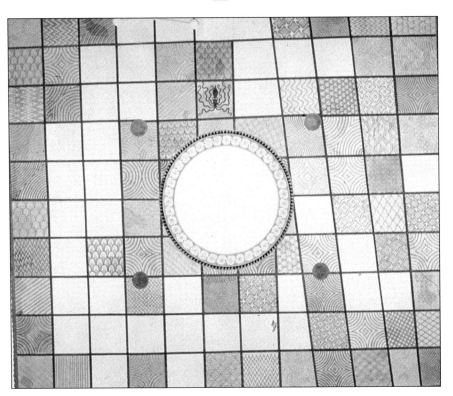

Figure 7. Painted patterns on floor and hearth, throne room

The hearth was also adorned with painted patterns (flames, notches, and spirals) on the riser, a narrow ledge, and the broad border that surrounded the place for the fire. Near the hearth, beside the western column base, stood a clay table of offerings, coated with stucco. The columns, with their thirty-two flutes, and all the woodwork of ceiling and balcony were no doubt brightly painted. All four walls were covered with frescoes. A preserved fresco of a lion and griffin comes from the wall to the left of the throne; it was probably matched by another pair to the right. Farther to the viewer's right on the same wall was a banquet scene, perhaps the culmination of a procession of men and women leading a bull to sacrifice, which begins in room 5. One of the most evocative fragments shows a male figure seated on a rock and playing a lyre (Fig. 8).

Figure 8. Fresco from throne room: the lyre player

Beside the throne, at the king's right, is a curious instal-
lation—a shallow basin-like hollow in the floor—from
which a narrow V-shaped channel leads to a second slightly
lower hollow some 2 m (6.5 feet) distant. It might have
been a convenience to permit the king, without getting
down from his throne, to pour out libations to one or another
of the gods, a ceremony often mentioned in the Homeric
poems.

The many open slots and grooves visible in the walls
surrounding the throne room once contained the great vertical and horizontal beams which in Mycenaean architec-
ture made up the sturdy framework of the walls. Originally
the beams may have been left visible in the face of the wall,
more-or-less in the fashion of the half-timbered style in
England; but in the later phases of the palace the timbers
were all covered over with plaster and could not be seen. It
is obvious that the wooden beams contributed much to the
intensity of the fire that destroyed the palace and turned so
many of its stones into lime.

Figure 9. Drinking cups (kylikes) in pantry 19

Figure 10. Pots of various sizes in pantry 18

Figure 11. Drinking cups (kylikes) in pantry 19

Figure 12. Bowls and small storage jar (pithos)
in pantry 21

Originally there seems to have been a long corridor on each side of the throne room giving access to many storerooms. The passage on the left, or southwestern, side was later divided by crosswalls into additional rooms (13, 16, 18, 22). The five small chambers (17, 19, 20, 21, 22) in the western corner of the building, found filled with crushed pottery, had clearly been pantries in which the main stock of ordinary household dishes of the palace was kept. The long narrow room (18), which may be seen close beside the inner half of the throne room, contained, in addition to many large pots of various shapes, numerous diminutive votive vessels, as well as part of a table of offerings (Fig. 10). The room (19) beyond at the left, which once had wooden shelving on all sides, contained—by actual count—2,853 tall-stemmed drinking cups, all crushed and shattered (Figs. 9, 11). The other three pantries were likewise filled

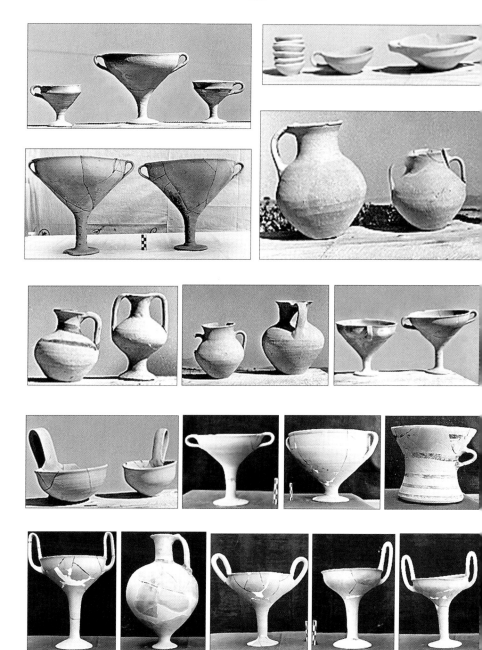

Figure 13. Pots from the pantries: representative shapes

with "china" of many sizes and at least twenty-three different shapes (Figs. 12, 13), and the total number of vases found in this quarter exceeded 6,000.

Directly behind the throne room are two fairly large storerooms (23, 24), where olive oil was kept in large jars that were set deep into stucco-coated stands (Fig. 14). There were seventeen jars in room 23 and sixteen in room 24. Many tablets and fragments of tablets found in room 23, scattered about on the stand and on the floor, indicate that various types of perfumed olive oil were stored here; it is of interest to note that the word for olive oil, ELAIWON, which appears on the tablets, is essentially the same as that used in Classical Greek, and even modern Greek, today, more than 3,000 years later.

A long corridor (25, 28, 35) still survives on the northeastern side of the throne room. Through a branch passage (26) it gave access to yet another oil storeroom (27) in the northern corner of the building, where remains of sixteen large jars were found still in place. Opposite the throne room to the northeast is a suite of five chambers (30, 31, 32, 33, 34) of various sizes. The northwesternmost (32) likewise contained olive oil in a dozen jars, and there were numerous

Figure 14. Main Building from northwest, with rooms 23 and 24 in foreground

Figure 15. Painted pots from room 32

smaller vessels of other kinds. Many of these pots are of a distinctive shape, and the painted decoration is unusually elaborate for this site (Fig. 15); it is likely that the most elegant grade of oil was kept here. Some of the oil at least was perfumed, as three tablets found in the room confirm. The other rooms in the suite seem to have been empty on the day of the fire, or were used for the storage of perishable materials, but well above the floor in the middle chamber (31) were found many small fragments of ivory, burned and blackened by fire and badly broken, which had obviously fallen from the room above. Recent research suggests they are fragments of furniture inlay.

Farther along in the corridor, almost directly opposite the door from the vestibule in front of the throne room, eight stone steps of a stairway (36) that led to the upper floor are still preserved in situ. Measurements of the steps and of the space available for the stairway indicate that the flight originally consisted of some twenty-one steps to the level above. On the opposite side of the building, also probably approached by a door from the vestibule, remains of two steps of another staircase (14–15) have survived. On this side the stairway rose to a landing in nine steps, turned to the right in two or three steps to another landing, then again to the right in a further flight of nine or ten steps to a corridor in the upper story. The level of the upper story was approximately 3.25 m (11 feet) higher than that of the ground floor.

The long corridor (35) continues beyond the north-eastern staircase and opens into a passage (37) that turns to the left, opposite the great portico (4) in front of the throne room. Here one enters a lobby (38) from which two rooms on the left are accessible (39–40). They contained little of note save two or three interesting pots. Another door from the lobby leads straight ahead to a gateway (41), which had a single wooden column standing on a stone base in its façade.

The latter opened northeastward onto a fairly spacious walled court (42), paved with stucco. This court was a late addition to the building; the rough stone walls forming it are very different in character from the finely smoothed blocks of the external wall of the building. We do not know what the court was used for; Blegen and Rawson thought it might have been the king's private court, in keeping with their view that the Main Building was a royal residence. More recent scholars, however, regard the entire complex as more administrative than residential. When excavated, this court was full of pottery that had been broken and discarded, including at least 348 shattered drinking cups, suggesting it was used partly as a refuse dump in the final stage of the life of the palace. In earlier phases there was probably a road or street that led from this gateway to the northeastern end of the site. In the late wall, which had no outside entrance or exit, there is, almost opposite the portal, a small squarish opening in which may be seen a terracotta water pipe. It thus seems likely that running water was brought to the site. There are no traces to show that a permanent water basin was installed in the court; perhaps a jar full of water was left standing here.

Beyond the northwestern end of the court one sees the only surviving part of the building's original exterior wall. It has an outside face made of large squared blocks of limestone, but with peculiar open V-shaped joints. All the blocks of the second course from the bottom bear on their top surface holes for dowels by which was fastened a great horizontal wooden beam, perhaps as much as 30 cm (1 foot) thick. Some four or five courses higher there was probably another beam of the same kind, running along the length of the wall. If there were window openings, the existence of which is uncertain, the lower beam could have served as a sill and the upper beam as the lintel. Just to the northwest, beyond the court, there is a rather broad recess or niche in the wall, probably designed for aesthetic reasons; perhaps it contained a window. Outside the wall, farther northwestward, a large spread of squared blocks that fell from the wall has been left just as it was found. Looking from the court one can distinguish five or six rows of these stones, each probably representing a course. It is clear that a large section of the wall fell outward in one piece as a unit when the fire

Figure 16. Ruins of the lobby

that consumed the palace was at its height. The olive oil stored in storeroom 32 may well have burst into flame with explosive violence.

Regaining the lobby (38) we may pause to note that it was found filled with the crushed wreckage of some twenty or more large storage jars (pithoi) and many smaller pots (Figs. 16, 17). The pithoi had contained olive oil and had for the most part fallen from the upper floor; their flammable contents clearly roused the flames to destructive fury.

Figure 17. Large storage jars (pithoi) and other pots

Scattered about in the burned debris were found nineteen fragments of inscribed tablets, which deal with olive oil of various kinds and for various purposes.

Passing southeastward through a doorway one enters a long, narrow bathroom (43), the only one of its kind yet found in a Mycenaean palace on the Greek mainland with its equipment still fairly well preserved. A terracotta bathtub (larnax) stands against the southeastern wall of the room. It is decorated with painted patterns, and set into a stucco-coated base made of clay. The tub is rather short; the bather presumably sat in it while a servant or attendant poured water over him.[12] A convenient step of clay, coated with stucco, made it easy to step from the floor into the bath. In the southern corner of the room, on the same side as the bath, is a tall stand also made of clay coated with plaster. In it were set two large storage jars (pithoi) some 1.20 m (4 feet) high, which probably contained the water needed for the bath. In the bottom of the southwestern pithos were found seven, and in that of the other jar nine, plain drinking cups, along with a few other small pots. One complete drinking cup was discovered on the bottom of the bath itself. These vessels were no doubt used for pouring water over the bather.

Returning through the lobby and the passage to the main corridor, and going out through a doorway on the left, one enters a small colonnade (44), which had a façade of two wooden columns fronting on the palace court (Fig. 5). They stood on stone bases, and each had a decorative stucco ring around its lower end. The impressions in the stucco show that each column had sixty flutings. The columns must have supported a balcony from which people could look out over the court, with a good view of the ceremonies that no doubt often took place there on state occasions.

At the southeastern end of this stoa are two doorways. The one to the right led to a stairway (54), which still retains three steps and part of a fourth; it ascended to the upper story of a tower-like structure (55–57) beside the propylon (Fig. 18). This may have been the lookout station or the headquarters of the palace guard. The other doorway,

Figure 18. View north across tower and queen's quarters

on the left, opened into a further corridor (45) from which one could turn left into a rather large and elegant room (46) with a hearth and frescoed wall decoration. Because it was a smaller version of the throne room (6) in these respects, Blegen dubbed it the queen's hall. It suffered great damage from the fire, no doubt intensified by the olive oil stored on the floor above in the jars that fell into the lobby (38); the oil had spread out into the bath and probably also the adjacent room. The floor of hall 46, which may once have possessed painted decoration, was badly damaged and blackened, and the stones in the walls were calcined. The plaster bearing wall paintings fell in fragments to the floor. Enough has been recovered, however, to show that zoological scenes were favored, with representation of griffins, life-sized lions or lionesses, and other animals, probably on all four walls (Fig. 19). The hearth in the center of the room,

Figure 19. Griffin and lion fresco from queen's hall

though much smaller than that in the throne room, was decorated in the same manner, but more delicately, with flame patterns, zigzags, and spirals (Fig. 20). Four or five successive coats of stucco can be counted, each with painted decoration.

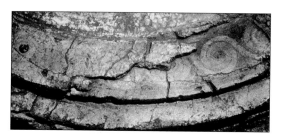

Figure 20. Painted patterns on small hearth in queen's hall

A doorway in the northeastern corner of the room led into another walled court (47), similar to the adjacent so-called king's court (42) and like it a late modification to the original building plan, which could not be entered from outside. On the pavement, near the door, were found near-ly three dozen painted stirrup jars of various sizes.[13] Two or three rows of smallish holes aligned across the court might have served for posts to fence off parts of the area. They may have supported an awning to shade part of the enclosure, or a line on which to hang up laundry, or shelving for industrial purposes. The uses to which the court was put cannot be recovered, but the debris found in it suggests that in the final years of the palace's existence it served a humbler purpose than was originally intended for this area.

Another doorway from the queen's hall led into a cor-ridor (48) from which a branching passage (49) gave access to a small room (50) in the corner of the building. The walls were decorated with frescoes, unfortunately very badly da-maged by the fire, and the floor was divided into squares, seven rows of seven, delicately painted with linear patterns as well as with semirealistic octopuses, dolphins, and other fish in alternating squares (Figs. 21, 22). The narrow pas-sage also had painted decorations on its floor with an octo-pus and linear patterns.

Figure 21. Detail of octopus in floor fresco, room 50

Figure 22. Detail of dolphins and fish in floor fresco, room 50

Figure 23. Stirrup jars

A neighboring room to the southwest (53), accessible only by going around through the corridor (51–52) and entering from the southwest, was possibly a lavatory. Seventeen stirrup jars (Fig. 23) stood on the floor to the left of the door, and near the eastern corner water could run down through an opening in a large stone slab to an underground drain.

SOUTHWESTERN BUILDING

Going out again through the main propylon of the building and turning to the right in court 58, just to the southwest of the archives complex, one comes to an ascending ramp (59) with stucco floor (Fig. 24). On the left is a fairly long narrow room (60), which was found to contain a store of 850 or more pots of some twenty-five different shapes (Fig. 25). Most of them had apparently been stacked on wooden shelves, but the larger vessels were set on the floor, one inside another, and many were recovered intact (Fig. 26).

Continuing on past this pantry one turns to the left, passing through a doorway (61), and after a few steps comes to a second doorway to the right; this opens into a broad

Figure 24. Ascending ramp with stucco floor

Figure 25. Stucco floor, location of larger vessels in room 60

Figure 26. Pots of various shapes from room 60

Figure 27. Columns of the large entrance hall 64

court (63) paved with stucco. The passage once continued on southwestward down the slope, but beyond this gateway only the foundations of the walls survive. An extensive area on the southwestern slope of the hill was for a long period used as a quarry by seekers of building materials, who have pillaged the ruins and added vastly to the damage caused much earlier by the disastrous fire.

Turning through the gateway mentioned, one enters the broad court (63), and crossing it one reaches a large entrance hall (64) which had two columns in its façade (Fig. 27). They were made of wood and set up on stone bases, which still survive. The columns were fluted, as shown by the impressions in the stucco floors that were laid up against the lower ends of the shafts. The flutings seem to have been forty-four in number. This entrance hall was of considerable size, more than 7 m (22.75 feet) wide and 10 m (32.5 feet) long. Its outer wall toward the northeast was built of large squared blocks, laid in even courses, with occasional horizontal timbers. The hall was paved with stucco, which may have borne painted decoration, though none can now be seen. The walls were coated with plaster of good quality,

Figure 28. Frieze of hunting dogs, hall 64

decorated with frescoes. A good deal of it belonging to the lowest course of the wall was found still in place. Above it, as shown by abundant fallen fragments that lay on the floor, was a long frieze of hunting dogs (Fig. 28). The room had a single interior column, which stood on a stone base. The latter was set along the longitudinal axis of the room occupying a most peculiar position: it is opposite the middle of the broad entrance on the southeast and a doorway in the northwestern wall, and it is in line with a wider doorway that leads into a great hall toward the southwest. One wonders how beams resting on the column were supported at the other end. A stand for a sentry beside the doorway to the southwest indicates that the large hall beyond was probably the chief room of state (65).

This too had a stucco floor, but it is preserved to a width of only a meter or two. Beyond that it is missing, because of erosion that has carried away the rest of the floor and much below it. Inside the hall on the right as one enters, one stone column base is still in situ. Three circular foundations that once supported similar bases complete a group of four. This was obviously the principal room in the southwestern wing of the palace, which may be slightly older than the Main Building. The hall, with its four or probably six columns, must have been the throne room in the earlier phase. No trace of a hearth was found, since the erosion mentioned has carried away the deposit well below the floor. The hall might have had two lateral balconies rather than one running around all four sides of the room. In this arrangement of a spacious entrance hall and then a turn to the left into the throne room we may have a Mycenaean palace plan earlier than the one that later became normal, which has all the principal rooms following one after another along the same axis.[14] This throne room had no other entrance except the doorway opening to the northeast.

Behind the entrance hall a much smaller doorway opened northwestward into a lobby (66). Immediately to the left there was a stairway (69) to an upper story, as indicated by a small fragment of the lowest step. To the right a doorway gave access to a short passage (67) and thence northwestward into a very small room (68). This was a pantry, in which were recovered some three hundred vessels, for the most part cooking pots, some standing on three legs; notable are two large circular pans, braziers, and many deep two-handled jars.

Returning to the lobby and passing through another doorway into another passage (70) running to the left, one turns northwestward and enters a fairly large apartment (71), which had a small side chamber (72) toward the northeast beside it. The large room contained little of interest. On the stone threshold of the small chamber were found five inscribed tablets that had been almost melted by the heat of the fire that destroyed the building. Behind these two rooms is a long narrow space (76) walled in on all sides. Perhaps it was a light well to provide air for these two rooms.

Going back to the passage (70) and turning to the right (southwest) one comes to a doorway that opens into another fairly large lobby (73). Beyond it straight ahead through yet another door is a room (74) of which virtually nothing is now left. Northwest of the lobby is a complex of passages (75, 79) with five doorways close together that led into successive small chambers. One of them to the right (78) may have been a bathroom, since a drain pipe, cut in stone, apparently led out at floor level through the northwest wall.

In a separate building of considerable size just outside to the north of this bathroom may probably be recognized the wine cellar of the southwest wing. The plan shows one large room (82), but excavations to the northwest led Blegen to suppose that the building had another room of equal size on this side, and may have continued to the northeast as well. Subsequently the complex was replaced by another group of rooms (83–86). The greater part of the floor is missing in room 82, but the bottoms of several jars, sunk deeply into the ground along the southeastern wall, support its identification as a wine storage building.

Going back to the Southwestern Building one may recognize two apartments (80, 81) that occupy the western corner, but the erosion on this side of the hill has carried away virtually all the remains of the floor and nothing can be said as to the character of this quarter.

The westerly angle of the building resembles a massive projecting tower. What is left of it seems to be only the substructure built of large stone slabs, for the most part not worked at all. The superstructure above the level of the floor was, however, almost surely built in its outer face of squared blocks of poros, many fragments of which were found lying outside the wall. This angle both on its northwestern face and on its southwestern side, where it shows two characteristic projecting offsets, is a massive and impressive structure. Whether it was visible in part or covered with earth at the time the palace was occupied is not certain. This wall, or substructure, formed the outer limit of the Southwestern Building. Behind the throne room with its four or six columns the wall was immensely thick, but only the lowest courses of the foundation of the outer face are now preserved. For here the poros blocks, which were evidently laid to a much deeper level than in the northwesterly section, have all been removed by looters in search of building material.

To the southeast, beyond the throne room, the destruction carried out by plunderers was even more thorough, and not enough remains of the further extension of the building to allow a certain reconstruction of the plan. The outside wall, built with a face of ashlar blocks, has been stripped bare except for a chance survival here and there. It continued some distance toward the southeast, then turned sharply toward the northeast, then swung once again to the southeast for 12 m (40 feet) or more, then turned again northeastward; how it ended is not yet certain, nor can the various rooms and apartments contained in it be clearly differentiated. It is likely in any case that the building ended approximately in line with the front of the central block.

The Southwestern Building is probably the oldest element in the palace. The confusing ruins on the southwestern slope of the hill indicate that there were at least two destructions by fire followed by rebuilding, and the disturbance has been made the worse by systematic as well as casual quarrying among the ruins. In the debris two Frankish coins were found, showing that the looting began at least as early as the 13th century. There was also a copper coin (soldo) of Venice of about 1700 and two Turkish coins of the 18th century. The removal of stone continued until modern times; a vast amount of material is said to have been taken from the site in the early 1890s when the main road was built.

NORTHEASTERN BUILDING

The Northeastern Building of the palace is separated from the central block and the two courts beside it by a broad ramp paved with stucco (91). It is a fairly large structure, comprising six rooms and a passage, and perhaps a roofed portico with a colonnade (Fig. 39). Entering opposite the eastern angle of court 47, one sees on the left a small, almost square, room (93), open across its front, between two massive anta blocks. The floor was so near the surface of the ground that it has been plowed away. Set in the stucco floor in front of this façade (92) is a rectangular stone base, plastered on all four sides and on top, and decorated with painted patterns similar to those at the bottom of the wall in the southwestern entrance hall. This base may have been an altar, and the small room facing it was perhaps a shrine.

Among the hundred and more fragments of tablets found in this building, one mentions a goddess Potnia Hippeia, Mistress of Horses.

To the northeast of the altar are two stone foundations, which may have supported columns of a porch, aligned with the northeastern wall of the shrine. Entering the portico (94) and turning to the left, one traverses a broad passage (95) which was found to contain little or nothing except a jar or pithos in its northern corner. Opposite this, on the left, a doorway opens into a small chamber (96). In the entrance was recovered a large stemmed krater (mixing bowl) with painted decoration, but the use of the room is not known. Proceeding on to the northwest the passage may have ended in a doorway leading out. To the left is a room (97) occupying the west corner of the building. Deep down below its floor was found a well-built stone-lined shaft, possibly a Middle Helladic grave that existed before the Northeastern Building was erected.

Across the passage to the right one enters a still larger rectangular room (98) occupying the northern corner of the workshop. It was probably a storeroom for supplies of raw materials, and it produced two large jars and many small pots along with numerous fragments of bronze and twenty-one clay sealings (Fig. 29). These are small lumps of clay that bear impressions made by sealstones or signet rings. The room had only the one entrance. Going out by it and turning to the left through the same broad passage one reaches a doorway on the left that opens into the largest of all the apartments (99) in the workshop. Like all the rooms in this structure, it had a floor of clay. On it in the north-western half of the room were found eleven complete and four fragmentary clay sealings and some ninety-seven inscribed tablets and fragments of tablets, which when joined together and mended were reduced to about half that number. Many of them deal with repairs in leather or in metal. Others mention parts of chariots. Yet others refer to supplies of leather or bronze expected or received. This inscriptional evidence is sufficient to establish the character of the building as a workshop.

Figure 29. Clay sealings

To the southeast below this long hall was another room
(100), probably forming the east corner of the structure and
corresponding to room 98 on the north. Only its northwestern and northeastern walls are preserved, but the bed-
ding trench of the southeastern wall clearly determines the
limit of the room and probably of the building. Most of
the actual floor is missing, but deposits within the area
yielded hundreds of diminutive bronze arrowheads and a
great many small fragments of ivory, some bearing remains
of incised decoration. Some arrowheads were also found in
front of the shrine to the southeast of the altar.

The Northeastern Building was the latest Mycenaean
addition to the palace complex, postdating courts 42 and 47
and the ramp (91). The foundations are of rubble, and the
superstructure of the walls was built of crude brick, un-
doubtedly laid within a heavy wooden framework. This
building, like all the other elements of the palace, was destroyed in the great fire.

Passing the altar again and turning northwestward, one
walks up the stucco-paved ramp (91) between the workshop and the two enclosed courts beside the Main Building.

Alongside the wall on the right is a U-shaped water channel, cut in stone blocks, which carried off the surplus water from a fountain at the top of the ramp just opposite the western corner of the workshop. Here is the terminus of an aqueduct which brought running water to this place. The line of the aqueduct has been traced northeastward to the far edge of the hill. At the place where the water was delivered, there seem to have been several branching channels, one going northwestward toward a reservoir (102), another being carried by a pipe through the wall of the northwesterly court (42), and a third heading southeastward to what Blegen called the fountain. The actual source of the water is probably to be sought in a spring called Rouvelli, which still exists beside the asphalt road about 1 km to the northeast of the site. The aqueduct must have been carried across an intervening valley, probably by means of a wooden trestle. Along the line of the aqueduct on the palace hill there are at least two settling basins, shaped much like the bathtub in the bathroom of the palace. There is another to the northwest of court 42, and a fourth stands behind the central block of the palace. Still another, represented only by fragments, was found in room 71 in the southwestern wing. How these tubs that were not connected with the aqueduct were filled with water is not clear.

WINE MAGAZINE

Outside the Main Building, to the north and parallel to the steep northwestern edge of the hill, is the storage building that Blegen called the Wine Magazine. A doorway on its northern side led into an anteroom (104) from which one could enter a very large room (105) containing storage jars. Four rows, one along the southeastern wall, two down the middle of the hall, and fragments of another running along the northwestern wall, contained more than thirty-five capacious jars. Many of them still stand in their original position, though all are cracked or broken, and, since they appear just below the surface of the ground, most have lost their rims and necks through the action of the plow.

Some sixty or more clay sealings were found in this building; four of them bear the sign for wine in the Linear B script. These sufficed to give the building its name, but some of the jars may have held other substances. The impressions had been stamped on lumps of clay wrapped around strings or cords that tied on the lids or stoppers of the wineskins or other containers that were brought here. In this way the senders had certified the kind or vintage or source of each skin or jar. The sealings were in the doorway between the storeroom itself and the anteroom, where they were discarded when they had served their purpose.

NORTHEASTERN PART OF CITADEL

As mentioned above, the northeastern part of the hilltop was apparently left open and unoccupied by buildings during the time the palace flourished (Fig. 2). Toward the northeastern edge, however, a complex of walls has been exposed, most of which belongs to Early Mycenaean times before the palace was built. What is left looks like a relatively narrow street, lined on each side with house walls running from north to south. These walls seem to have survived because they lie in a slight hollow in the hilltop and were consequently not demolished when the northeasterly section of the hill was leveled off, perhaps in preparation for building the palace.

Farther to the north in the abrupt edge of the hill remains of a gateway have been uncovered. The approach ascends steeply in a broad roadway paved with large stone slabs, laid almost in a step-like system. The gateway led through a circuit wall, scanty remains of which are still visible. Blegen traced the wall along the northwesterly scarp of the hill, but on the other side of the gateway to the southeast and south no certain remains have yet been recognized. On the evidence of the pottery found, the gateway and the contiguous sections of the wall must be assigned to the beginning of the Early Mycenaean period, Late Helladic I. This portal and the wall were apparently destroyed before the palace of Late Helladic IIIB was built.

Figure 30. Floor of tholos tomb

THOLOS TOMBS

About a hundred yards to the northeast through an olive grove one reaches a tholos tomb, the dome of which was restored in 1957 by the Greek Archaeological Service.[15] Though built mainly of small flat stones, it is a large tomb with a diameter of 9.35 m, or roughly 30.5 feet. The tomb had collapsed and had become filled up to the top of the lintel. It had evidently been plundered in antiquity and was found thoroughly disturbed from top to bottom, but the looters had been unusually careless and much valuable material was left to be recovered. The objects found comprise numerous items of gold, including a gold seal bearing the representation of a winged griffin, two rings, ornaments in the form of small owls, and a shield-shaped pendant; also 250 beads of amethyst and still more of amber, an amethyst gem and several other sealstones, fragments of bronze weapons, etc.

Remains of another tomb, published as a "Grave Circle" but probably also a tholos, lie almost equidistant toward the south from the palace hill.[16] Almost the whole vault had been cut away down to within 30 cm (12 inches) of the floor, but a considerable part of the floor was found undisturbed (Fig. 30). In six untouched pits or shafts beneath it were unearthed a great many valuable objects including four large jars (each containing a skeleton), twenty-two swords and daggers of bronze, several bronze vessels, a large collection of pottery, and a magnificent sealstone representing a wild boar at bay.

About 1 km down the road toward the plain is yet another tholos tomb that likewise must have had some connection with the palace site.[17] It was excavated in 1939. This too was found to have been looted, but numerous objects had been overlooked by the robbers, including many pieces of carved ivory and beads of gold, semiprecious stone, and glass paste.

A cemetery of chamber tombs for the ordinary people, who lived in the lower town that surrounded the acropolis, has been found on the slopes of a ridge some 500 m (550 yards) to the west of the palace.[18] Three tombs have been excavated, yielding some good pottery and other objects. Two of the vaults were found in a collapsed state and have been refilled with earth.

IDENTIFICATION AND DATE OF THE PALACE

The palace, as it has now been revealed, with its five chief buildings, is a work of the 13th century, and its history falls between 1300 and 1200 B.C. The complex is spread out over a fairly extensive area as large as, if not larger than, that occupied by other palaces of the same period on the Greek mainland. In its size and arrangement the central building takes its place alongside the contemporary establishments at Mycenae and Tiryns. It exhibits the same general plan in its entrance gateway, court, portico, vestibule, and throne room, with interior columns arranged around a central hearth. It is obvious that it was built by a ruler of great wealth and political power.

No king is definitely identified in the inscribed tablets that have been found in this palace, but Greek tradition tells of a Mycenaean royal dynasty in western Messenia, the

Neleids. According to myth Neleus, a royal prince from Thessaly, came and acquired the site, and his son Nestor succeeded him and ruled through three generations of men. Nestor, who took part in the expedition against Troy, provided and equipped ninety vessels, second only to the one hundred ships of the expedition leader, Agamemnon himself. Nestor returned in safety from Troy and survived a good many years. He was succeeded by a son and grandson, perhaps even by a great-grandson. The palace was captured and put to the torch by the Dorians and was totally destroyed. The inhabitants fled. Some of the Neleids took refuge in Athens, where they founded some of the leading Athenian families; others went to Asia Minor and settled in Ionia. Whatever its later history, the site of Pylos never again reached the same level of culture. Indeed, in the Classical period no one knew exactly where Pylos had stood. But all the Greek writers who mention Nestor regarded him as a Messenian. The name Pylos survived into Classical times and later, attached to the fortress and region on the north side of the Bay of Navarino.

In the past fifty years archaeology has done much to confirm the historical reality of some of the personalities recorded by the epics and Greek folk memory as dominating the great Mycenaean centers. If there ever was a Nestor, surely he lived here in the palace at Englianos, which flourished in the 13th century. Even the name of "Pylos" fits: forty-six tablets from the site contain this place-name, sometimes written in large signs as a heading. The exact date when the palace was destroyed is not easily fixed to a year, but it occurred when Mycenaean pottery of the style called Late Helladic IIIB was reaching its end, and a few pieces of the succeeding style, Late Helladic IIIC, were beginning to appear. This was a time of great disturbance and destruction. Mycenae and Tiryns too were burned at the end of the pottery style LH IIIB, around 1200 B.C. Many other Mycenaean sites came to their end at the same time, such as Berbati, the Argive Heraeum, Zygouries, Thebes, and Gla, to mention only a few.

The cause of the destructions and abandonments remains a mystery, though there is increasing evidence that earthquakes hit some sites hard at this time, especially in the Argolid. At Pylos, however, there are signs of trouble well before the destruction took place. The palace complex underwent several alterations during the course of its history. The late addition of the Northeastern Building is just one of these. Storerooms were added also, both by new construction (27, 60, perhaps the wine magazine 104–105) and probably by conversion of existing rooms (32). Before the Northeastern Building was built, the creation of courts 42 and 47 had already blocked off access to the palace by an earlier entrance through gateway 41. Similarly, the construction of rooms 60–62 restricted access to the southwestern side of the complex, and corridor 18 was walled off at both ends so that pantries 19 and 20 no longer communicated with the rest of the Main Building. These increases in storage and workshop space, and the restriction of access to and circulation within the palace, indicate an increasingly centralized palace administration, and the anticipation of trouble either locally or from further afield. The violent burning destruction suggests that these concerns were justified.

(CWB and MR, JLD and CWS)

INVESTIGATIONS IN THE VICINITY OF THE PALACE OF NESTOR

Much is known about prehistoric settlements and cemeteries in the area that surrounds the Palace of Nestor. Kourouniotis and Christophilopoulos began an inventory of archaeological sites. Blegen and Dionysios Androutsakis, his excavation foreman, located others. In the 1950s and 1960s, their colleague William McDonald expanded investigations to Messenia as a whole by organizing a systematic program of reconnaissance, the University of Minnesota Messenia Expedition. In 1992–1995, parts of western

Figure 31. Beylerbey Ridge

Messenia were reexamined still more intensively by the Pylos Regional Archaeological Project. All these endeavors now allow the Palace of Nestor to be viewed in its regional context.

The Palace of Nestor is today approached from the parking lot to its southeast, but in ancient times the main route from the west coast may have followed the valley bottom to the north, not the course of the asphalt road to Chora. A chainlink fence encloses the principal palatial buildings but excludes less monumental remnants of the surrounding settlement. Relationships between this "Lower Town" and the cemeteries associated with the Palace of Nestor are clear. The chamber tombs mentioned by Blegen and Rawson were dug near the edge of the settlement; the remains of other tombs have been located in the intervening years. In contrast, Tholos IV lay well within the limits of the later Mycenaean town. All three tholos tombs were built at a time when the settlement was smaller and less compact, several centuries before the Palace of Nestor.

Several other Mycenaean sites are located only short distances from the Palace of Nestor and are worth a brief visit. We provide directions to those that are officially open to the public and are marked by signs. Several other contemporary sites are mentioned in passing.

Figure 32. Tholos tomb at Charatsari

Koryphasion　The low ridge called Beylerbey rises to the south of the village of Koryphasion (Fig. 31). Christophilopoulos brought this important Mycenaean site to the attention of Blegen, who visited it before beginning excavations at the Palace of Nestor. Many years later Marinatos found that the ridge is badly eroded and that soft marl bedrock lies almost immediately beneath the plowzone. But members of the Pylos Regional Archaeological Project have been able to estimate that settlement once covered five hectares (12 acres), an area a quarter as great as that associated with the Palace of Nestor.

North of Beylerbey, on the outskirts of Koryphasion, one can locate with some difficulty the tholos at Charatsari, excavated in 1926 by Kourouniotis (Fig. 32).[19] The latest pottery dates to the 15th century B.C. The tholos tomb appears to have been built toward or at the end of the Middle Bronze Age (ca. 1680 B.C.) and is thus the earliest of its type yet discovered in Greece. The tomb is located in a flat field, almost entirely buried underground. Dead were buried in pits and in large jars, the former with lavish offerings of vessels in precious metals and bronze weapons.

Figure 33. Palaionavarino and Cave of Nestor from Voidokoilia

Voidokoilia   The shallow sea inlet surrounded by sand dunes west of Osmanaga Lagoon is called Voidokoilia (in Greek, "ox-belly") Bay because of its distinctive shape.[20] At its western side rises the medieval fortress of Pylos at Palaionavarino (Old Navarino). On its northern slope, in the so-called Cave of Nestor (Fig. 33), excavations have recovered Neolithic pottery of the 4th millennium B.C. and of the Mycenaean period. On the rocky headland at the south end of Voidokoilia Bay are preserved the foundations of buildings that belong to the ancient Greek settlement of Coryphasion.[21] Mycenaean pottery has been found beneath them, in the hollows of the bedrock.

For much more impressive prehistoric remains, visit the headland at the north end of Voidokoilia Bay (Fig. 34). Here Marinatos unearthed a small Early Mycenaean tholos tomb. Pausanias, a Greek traveler who visited the area in the 2nd century A.C., mentions a "monument" of Thrasymedes, one of the sons of King Nestor, and Marinatos believed that this was his final resting place. Two human skeletons remained inside; the complete carcass of a cow appears to have been included as a grave gift. Recent excavations by

Figure 34. Voidokoilia from Palaionavarino

George Korres of the University of Athens have now de-
monstrated that the tholos tomb was set into the remnants
of a small Early Bronze Age village, dating to the later 3rd
millennium B.C. Obsidian from the Cycladic island of Me-
los found in its buildings demonstrates the existence of
trade and contact with the wider Aegean world. At the end
of the 3rd millennium B.C. the promontory was transformed
into a cemetery. Eventually a circular mound of earth and
rubble about 1.5 m (nearly 5 feet) high was heaped up over
the walls of the settlement and large jars were set into it as
containers for human remains.

Romanou Traces of Mycenaean occupation have been
found within the modern town of Romanou. A short
distance to the northwest, a large flat-bottomed rectangular basin, ca. 200 × 300 m (650 × 975 feet) in a bend of the
Selas River may have been the port of the Palace of Nestor
in Mycenaean times, but is now entirely filled with silt.

Northeast of the village of Romanou, a low hill called
Viglitsa affords a commanding view of the coast. Two early
Mycenaean tholos tombs were built there (Fig. 35).[22] Korres

Figure 35. Interior of
tholos at Viglitsa

has recently clarified the history of this important site. The tombs appear to have been set into remains of earlier settlements, with traces of occupation of the 3rd and earlier 2nd millennium B.C. The earlier of the two tholos tombs was built in the 16th century, the second slightly later. Finds from the tombs include a seal depicting a winged griffin and a terracotta box of the 12th century B.C. with a rare representation of a prehistoric Greek warship.

Tragana   The village of Tragana sits near the western end of one of the principal ridges that slope down to the sea from the foothills of Mount Aigaleon. On its outskirts Marinatos excavated one room of a house that contained finds exclusively of the Early Mycenaean period.[23] The room contained triton shells and more than one hundred pottery vessels. Investigations by the Pylos Regional Archaeological Project suggest that this structure did not belong to a larger village or town. It is possible that the room was part of an isolated mansion, long abandoned by the time the Palace of Nestor was built.

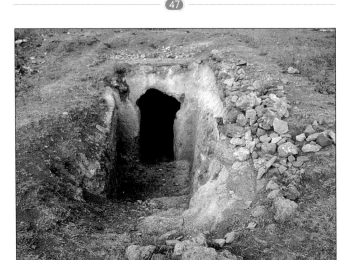

Figure 36. Entrance passage and door of southernmost chamber tomb at Volimidia

Chora The town of Chora is strategically situated at the junction of the ridge of Englianos and the expanse of flatter tableland that sits at the foot of Mount Aigaleon. It commands the only convenient routes leading north, south, or east from the Palace of Nestor. The earliest traces of occupation at Chora (4th millennium B.C.) were found by Marinatos in a cave called Katavothra not far south of the town square. Mycenaean remains are concentrated in the suburb known as Volimidia, along the asphalt road that leads ultimately to the village of Vlachopoulo. In 1953 Marinatos found occupation deposits contemporary with the Palace of Nestor and from Early Mycenaean times. He suspected that there had been a prosperous Mycenaean town at Volimidia. No true tholos tombs were ever built there. The site is best known for large chamber tombs, a third of them built already in the 16th century B.C. (Fig. 36). Many were reused in historical times.[24]

Myrsinochori The village of Myrsinochori is separated by a deep gorge from the uplands around Chora. Northeast of the village an earthen track leads along the ridge of Routsi to the village of Metamorphosis. No Mycenaean settlement has yet been found here, but two Early Mycenaean tholos tombs were discovered and excavated by Marinatos.[25] Both tombs were built long before the Palace of Nestor and had gone out of use by the 13th century B.C. Many of the luxury ornaments that adorned the burials have close parallels in the wealthy Shaft Graves at Mycenae of similar date, and one grave was exceptionally rich in amber beads. Other finds included bronze swords and daggers, vessels of precious metal, objects of ivory, and sealstones.

About a kilometer northeast of the Virgin of Routsi church, a team from the University of Athens under the direction of George Korres recently excavated a mound of stone and earth containing a large box-shaped grave constructed of stone slabs. Several burials were deposited in large storage jars along the periphery of the mound, with their mouths framed by stone slabs so as to form a threshold and lintel with door jambs. It has been suggested that the first tholos tombs monumentalized in stone this earlier form of interment.

(JLD)

LIFE IN MYCENAEAN PYLOS

Pylos was one of a number of kingdoms that flourished in Greece in the 14th and 13th centuries B.C. We do not know to what degree, if any, they were politically interconnected, but the inscribed tablets (Fig. 4), labels, and sealing nodules (Fig. 29) found at each center give us some information about the internal administrative structure and economic affairs of a Mycenaean kingdom. Pylos, with about one thousand tablets, has the lion's share of longer and more complete texts.

Since Ventris' discovery in 1952 that the tablets were in an early form of Greek, they have added a new dimension to our understanding of Mycenaean culture. From them we know that the Late Bronze Age inhabitants of Pylos and other centers organized the production of items that do not turn up in the archaeological record, like cloth and scented oil. The Mycenaeans kept track of different breeds of oxen, collected taxes, and worshiped many of the gods we know from classical Greece, such as Zeus, Poseidon, Hera, Ares, and Dionysos. Pylos managed a large labor force, paid in figs and grain by the central administration: shepherds and weavers, perfume boilers, bronzesmiths, and bath attendants. The administrative hierarchy is also well documented, from the ruler, called by the Homeric word for king, *wanax,* down to the district officials, and the menial labor force that kept the kingdom running smoothly.

Mycenaean social structure is less well understood. Individuals named in the tablets are elite members of society, while lower ranking workers are mentioned only as groups. There are references to slaves also, but here a word of caution is in order. Tablets from Pylos and Knossos show that slaves could be bought and sold, but also that they could own land and large flocks of sheep and goats, and that they received rations and made contributions to the gods in quantities comparable to nonslaves. The same ambiguity applies to other modern labels like "king" and "palace": it is important to remember that the Mycenaean significance of such terms probably did not correspond exactly with ours.

These tablets are nothing like the voluminous and varied records known from the Near East. They preserve no laws, no literature, no diplomatic or private correspondence; just lists of taxes and payments, goods stored, and goods offered to the gods. Furthermore, the tablets were never intended as permanent records, and they refer to the business of a single year. They were not even intentionally baked; we possess only those that were accidentally preserved when fire destroyed the palace. Thus we have records of only the final year of any palace administration. There are month names, but only occasional references like "last year's debt" and "the bronzesmiths will pay another year." It seems clear that tablets were not kept after the current year was up; any information worth retaining longer could have been transferred to a less bulky material like leather, as we

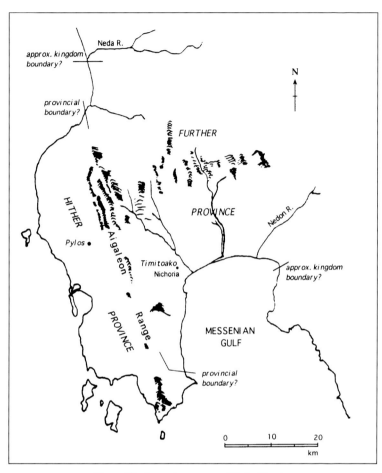

Figure 37. Approximate area of Pylos kingdom

know was the Minoan practice, or to a new year's set of tablets. We do, on the other hand, know that any topic ap-
pearing in these records is sure to be palace business.
Literacy in the Mycenaean world was confined to a rather
small number of people. Just twenty-six scribes have been
identified by their handwriting at Pylos (and another
eighteen groups of tablets may each represent a separate
scribal hand). So far, writing is not attested for any purpose other than economic administration. Despite the li-
mitations of this written evidence, by considering what the
tablets say, where they were found, and what was found with

them we can retrieve a good deal of information about the activities a palace administration controlled.

The Pylos kingdom covered about 2,000 square km (775 square miles), and may have extended throughout modern Messenia (Fig. 37). It was divided for administrative purposes into two provinces, described on the tablets as "this side of Aigolaion" and "beyond Aigolaion." It seems obvious, particularly if you are standing at the palace, that the boundary between them is the mountain range clearly visible to the northeast (Fig. 18). This range, known to the later Greeks and Romans as Aigaleon, bisects the peninsula from northwest to southeast. The seven districts of the Pylian Hither Province and nine of the Further Province are listed in a fixed geographical order on several tablets, referring both to incoming taxes and to outgoing allocations from the palace.

One set of tax documents further reveals the relationships among the different districts. There is a tablet for each district, listing assessments and payments of six different commodities, as well as some exemptions. Not all the commodities have been identified: two are certainly a type of homespun cloth and oxhides, and honey and wax may be among the others. But they must be rather common and/or the quantities must be rather small, since all districts are required to contribute all six commodities. We have a basic understanding of how the tax system worked, though some details are still obscure. Palace administrators did not tax each district independently. Rather, they began by setting the provincial assessment, and within each province they grouped certain neighboring districts together so that the tax burden was allocated fairly among richer and poorer districts in each part of the kingdom. This proportional grouping has a wider significance as well. Allocations of pigs, wine, and hides by the palace to the districts show the same relative amounts for each fiscal group; this must be the basis of the whole economic administration of the kingdom.

This is not to say that the individual districts were beyond the direct interest of the palace. One tablet shows a hierarchy of administrators for each, including a governor

Figure 38. Nichoria, street in Area III

(koreter) and vice-governor *(prokoreter)*. Individual districts are recorded as contributing flax, or housing bronzesmiths or textile workers employed by the palace. One district center has even been excavated, if scholars are right in identifying it with the site of Nichoria, across the Aigaleon range (Fig. 38). This settlement, on a hilltop near modern Rizomilo overlooking the Messenian Gulf, prospered and declined with the palace. Its geographic position and excavated remains match all the characteristics we expect of this town based on information in the tablets.[26] As survey and excavation continue to fill in the map of settlements in the region, it is becoming possible to suggest other match-ups between sites on the ground and important towns mentioned in the tablets.

Who ran this system, and what can we tell about the haves and the have-nots within it? The tablets are particularly valuable in confirming the existence of the *wanax* (king), for unlike Egypt and most Near Eastern cultures, Mycenaean Greece gives us no artistic images of a king, no ruler iconography at all. But from the texts we know that the *wanax* was the highest ranking member of a ranked society. This is particularly clear from a landholding document, where the royal plot is three times the size of that owned by the next ranking figure, the *lawagetas* (his name should mean that he leads the people, perhaps in a military sense). Other officials appear on other landholding tablets; they seem to receive the benefit of land in return for service of some kind, and they can rent out shares in turn to other individuals.

When it comes to the king's functions, there is very little evidence, but we know he played a significant role in both religious and secular affairs. The archaeological evidence supports this conclusion. The state apartments (4–6) embody the public power and splendor of a palatial center (Fig. 6). Access to this area from the main southeast entrance is very straightforward, and fresco remains from the outer porch suggest that the ceremonial procession observed in room 5 may actually have begun at the southeast entrance, so that the procession on the wall guided and accompanied visitors to the throne room (6). The frescoes of banqueting and entertainment here (Fig. 8), the libation channel next to the throne, and an offering table near the hearth tie the king closely to ritual activities. The startling quantities of ordinary household pottery found in pantries nearby (19–22, Fig. 13) suggest the regular entertainment of large numbers of people. Communal feasting is a way in many cultures of demonstrating and maintaining authority, and this may have been so at Mycenaean Pylos as well. The practice may also have had a ritual dimension; several Pylos texts list foods that are apparently earmarked for such feasts. It has been suggested that the spacious open area (63, 88) between the Main and Southwestern Buildings would have been a good space for large banquets: plenty of room, and easy access to the stores of crockery in the pantries.

Another topic on which the tablets give us a good deal of information is industrial production. There are hints in the tablets that the palace may have hired some otherwise independent workers, and paid them on contract for their services. Much more commonly, however, those working for the palace were fully or partially dependent on it. The palace collected raw materials and distributed them to craftsmen, and in due course recorded the receipt of the finished product. Such is the case with bronze workers at Pylos. The palace administrators were also much concerned with textile production, especially linen but also wool. One series of tablets records the amount of flax that various places were required to contribute to the center. Another lists the groups of women who did the work of spinning, weaving, and decorating linen (and probably woolen) cloth, along with other menial workers like grain-grinders and bath attendants. Most of these women are concentrated at Pylos itself, where there were twenty-eight work groups comprising a preserved total of 377 women, but others are stationed elsewhere: seven groups (120 women) in the Hither Province, and fourteen groups (142 women) in the Further Province. A different scribe kept track of the groups working in each province; the tablets noted not only the number of workers but how many children they had with them. Still another scribe noted the monthly rations of figs and grain for the Hither Province workers, but such records are not preserved for the Further Province groups.

The perfumed oil industry at Pylos is also a good example of how the center organized the production of important commodities. In the ancient world scented oil was a frequent offering to the gods, and it was also used for medicinal and cosmetic purposes. It was of particular value in a world without soap, where odors could be masked more easily than erased. The Mycenaean world relied for such purposes on olive oil scented with various fragrances. The jars which contained this oil are distinctive (Fig. 15: top center, middle right, and bottom left; Fig. 23). They are called stirrup jars, because the handle resembles a stirrup, and they have a very small mouth, suitable for the small quantities used and easy to stopper. They turn up as offerings in tombs, and they are by far the most common type of Mycenaean pottery found outside Greece. Thus the manufacture and export of perfumed oil was big business, and there is a good deal of information about it in the tablets.

Lists of ingredients give us clues to the various types of perfumed oil and how they were made. Rose perfume, for example, was created by first boiling astringent herbs like

Figure 39. The Northeastern Building

cyperus and coriander in the olive oil, to break down its natural resistance to absorbing odors. Then rose petals were steeped in the oil—a later Greek recipe requires several days of steeping, at 1000 roses a day! Such ingredient lists were kept in the archives complex (7–8), but in the oil storerooms 23 and 32 Blegen found inventories and allocation records. These indicate some of the uses to which scented oil was put: it was offered to various gods, given out to the king and to servants, and used to treat textiles (a practice that makes linen, for example, supple and shining as well as sweet smelling).

Further information about scribal organization at Pylos comes from the Northeastern Building (Fig. 39). A fragmentary tablet found in room 98 lists chariot wheels. A different scribe recorded hides (some of them red) for reins and harnesses, and goats or goat hides, and still another listed hides for other purposes. Tablets listing the work groups assigned to various tasks (most clearly related to chariot equipment) are the product of two other scribes, while yet another keeps track of personnel coming in from the provincial districts. Thus a number of administrators were set to the task of monitoring this workshop. There are also references to some workers "at the seat" of the goddess Potnia ("Mistress") of Horses, and others in the service of a different Potnia, presumably elsewhere. One of these locations could be the shrine (room 93) beside which the workshop was built. From the other finds in the workshop it is clear that materials relating to the activities mentioned were at least stored here, and no doubt they were worked on here as well.

The building was a very late addition to the palatial complex, and was thus built to meet a specific need. It is both large and elaborate, with one particularly big room (99) and extra-wide doorways to rooms 98 and 99, suitable for bringing large equipment in and out. In addition, finds in the rooms complement the information on the tablets about what tasks were performed here: strips of metal may come from chariots, and bright red and yellow patches on the floors of rooms 97 and 98 may have been dye substances, recalling the textual references to red hides.

As in the case of the perfumed oil industry, there are close connections between the Northeastern Building and the central archive. One tablet from the archives complex notes the arrival of supplies destined for the "chariot workshop," thought to be a reference to this building. A tablet concerned with chariot wheels came from room 98, as just noted, but the rest of this series was found in the central archives. It is likely that those tablets were all written in the workshop, where chariot work took place, then moved to the archives complex for storage. In addition, two of the ration tablets found in the archives complex refer to slaves of men listed on a personnel record from the workshop. Thus, while work records were created and kept in the workshop itself, the central archive was heavily involved in supplying needed materials, doling out rations for the workers, and inventorying the results of workshop projects.

(CWS)

THE CHORA MUSEUM

Finds from the Palace of Nestor and nearby tombs are on display in the Chora Museum.[27] Here the visitor can see much of the material mentioned in this guide, along with plans and reconstruction drawings that bring the ruins of the site to life. In front of the museum stand two busts: one of Carl Blegen, and the other of the Greek archaeologist Spyridon Marinatos, who excavated a number of grave sites in the Pylos region.

In each room of the museum the cases along the wall are numbered counterclockwise, starting to the right of the doorway as one enters. An appendix summarizes the material case by case; here follows a briefer summary, mentioning only a few items likely to interest the nonspecialist.

Room 1 The Mycenaean pottery exhibited in room 1 covers the full span of time from the earliest Late Helladic period, ca. 1650 B.C., to the end of the palace age, ca. 1200 B.C. Also on display is some much later pottery of the Hellenistic and Roman periods (for example, CASE 1, *top shelf*), when some of the Volimidia tombs were used for cult rituals.

CASE 3, along the right-hand wall, shows the rich contents of two Early Mycenaean tholos tombs at Routsi near the village of Myrsinochori south of Chora. Tholos 2 was found unrobbed, a rarity in Mycenaean archaeology, and yielded swords, a dagger, and other equipment of bronze, as well as fine Early Mycenaean pottery (CASE 3, *bottom shelf*).

CASE 9 in the center toward the back of the room contains gold vessels and jewelry from three tholos tombs at Peristeria, on a hill just east of Kyparissia. Large cups with spiral decoration stand above decorative pieces of sheet gold in a variety of shapes (leaves, flowers, owls, etc.), some so small that a magnifying glass is needed to appreciate the fine workmanship that went into them. Some larger jars from Routsi and Peristeria are on display outside the cases; the designs show the influence of Minoan Crete.

Room 2   Room 2 of the museum is devoted to finds from the palace. A plan hanging in the doorway helps the visitor see where each item came from. Most striking as one enters is the large quantity of undecorated pottery, in contrast to the painted tomb finds in the first room—here one enters the workaday world of the living. CASE 10 to the right of the doorway and CASE 19 to its left are crowded with drinking cups and bowls from the pantries; some are twisted or blackened from the intensity of the fire that destroyed the palace. The portable clay offering table near the front of the room was found next to a column base in the throne room. It is of a type used for ritual offerings, so it ties the Mycenaean king closely to religious affairs.

Low cases against each wall (CASES 11 and 12 on the right, CASES 18 and 17 on the left) contain fresco fragments from the palace. These include the well-known lyre player from the throne room (CASE 17 on the left; Fig 8) and a lion and griffin that decorated the walls of hall 46 (CASE 11 on the right; Fig 19), as well as some delightful smaller fragments, like the small-scale head of a deer (CASE 12). Watercolor reconstructions on the walls, by the excavation artist Piet de Jong, bring the fragments together and recapture their original appearance. CASE 32 in the middle of the room to the left contains replicas of some of the Linear B tablets found at Pylos, along with other objects from the archives complex, including some miniature votive drinking cups and a Venetian coin. (A second Venetian coin found elsewhere on the hill is displayed here with its fellow.) Some of the elegant and unusual painted jars from the special storeroom 32 are in CASE 13 on the right-hand wall (Fig. 15).

Room 3   Various finds are on display in room 3. Near the front of the room against the right-hand wall are two fragments of an architectural feature known as horns of consecration. Such horns appear in Minoan Crete, in both palatial and cultic contexts, and occasionally in Mycenaean Greece; in room 2, CASE 12, a fresco fragment of a building shows them in position on top of a wall. The horn fragments were found built into the wall and floor of ramp 91, but we cannot tell how or where they were originally used. Dominating the back of the room is a huge storage jar that once stood in archives room 7, and in the back left corner are two large sections of the chimney from hall 46.

Some of the objects in the cases are from the palace buildings and from Blegen's excavations in the immediate vicinity, including trenches that reveal glimpses of the Mycenaean town of Pylos. Others come from tombs belonging to the site. The objects from the palace complex and settlement are mostly fragmentary, but they include some pieces of unusual beauty and interest. Two fragments of a stone vase in fine green Lacedaemonian stone (from nearby Sparta) in CASE 31, the freestanding case on the left, come from the area northeast of the palace complex. Parallels suggest that the vessel was shaped like a lion's head, but all that survives is part of the deftly carved mane.

On the bottom shelf of CASE 28 on the left are clay twists from room 23. They are the raw material of Linear B tablets, accidentally baked by the destruction fire, and they preserve the handprints of the scribe(s) who squeezed them into this shape. CASES 20, 21, and 29 hold grave goods from tombs associated with the palace site. Most complete is the assemblage from the unrobbed Vayenas tholos, called a "Grave Circle" in the site publication (see above). Among the finds are several swords that were deliberately bent before burial. This practice, known in Mycenaean Greece and elsewhere, may mark the end of the owner's career as a warrior.

(CWS)

APPENDIX
CONTENTS OF THE CHORA MUSEUM

ROOM 1

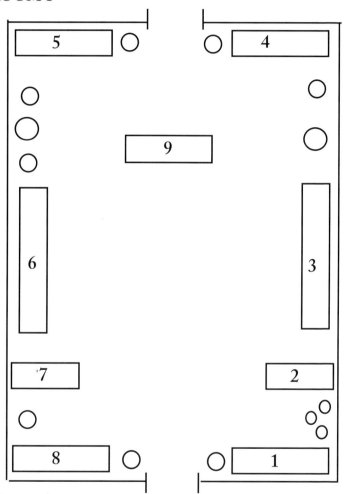

CASE I   Material from tombs at Volimidia

Top: Hellenistic and Roman pottery from Angelopoulos chamber tombs 4, 5, 7

Middle: Mycenaean pottery and other finds from Angelopoulos chamber tombs 8, 11

Bottom: Roman and Mycenaean pottery and Mycenaean spindle whorls from Volimidia tombs

CASE 2   Mycenaean material from
tombs at Volimidia

Top: Pottery and spindle whorls from
Vorias chamber tomb 1

Middle: Pottery and other finds from
Vorias chamber tombs 4, 7

Bottom: Pottery and other finds from
Vorias chamber tombs 3, 6

CASE 3   Material from Pylia and
Triphylia districts

Top: Casual finds of Mycenaean and
Protogeometric pottery, axes, and
other finds

Mycenaean pottery and other finds,
Hellenistic pottery from Papoulia
tholos 3

Middle: Pottery, weapons, scales, and
other finds from Routsi tholos 1
(Early Mycenaean)

Bottom: Pottery, weapons, and other
finds from Routsi tholos 2 (Early Mycenaean)

CASE 4   Material from Voroulia and
Volimidia

Top: Early Mycenaean pottery from
Tragana-Voroulia storeroom

Middle: Mycenaean pottery and other
finds from Kephalovryso shaft grave 1
at Volimidia

Bottom: Pottery and other finds from
Kephalovryso chamber tomb 3 and pit
grave at Volimidia

CASE 5   Material from Peristeria and
Tragana

Top: Pottery and other finds from
Peristeria hill, including some black-
glazed Hellenistic vessels

Middle: Pottery and other finds from
Peristeria hill

Bottom: Pottery, boars' teeth, sealstones

and other finds from Tragana tholos 1,
2, including a Hellenistic bowl and
lamp

CASE 6   Material from tombs at
Volimidia and Chora

Top: Pottery from Kephalovryso shaft
grave 2, chamber tombs 5, 6 at
Volimidia

Middle: Pottery and other finds from
Koronios chamber tombs 2, 3, 5, 6
at Volimidia

Bottom: Pottery and other finds from
Kephalovryso chamber tombs 4, 7;
Mastoraki chamber tomb 1 at
Volimidia; Ayios Elias chamber tomb
1 at Chora

CASE 7   Material from tombs at
Volimidia

Top: Pottery from Angelopoulos chamber
tomb 6

Middle: Pottery and other finds from
Angelopoulos chamber tomb 6

Bottom: Pottery and other finds from
Angelopoulos chamber tomb 7

CASE 8   Material from tombs at
Volimidia

Top: Mycenaean and Hellenistic pottery
from Angelopoulos chamber tombs
1, 2, 9, 10

Middle: Mycenaean and Protogeometric
pottery and other finds from
Angelopoulos chamber tomb 5

Bottom: Mycenaean and later pottery and
other finds from Angelopoulos
chamber tomb 4

CASE 9   Material from Peristeria tholos
1, 2, 3

Outside cases: Pottery from tombs at
Volimidia, Papoulia, Routsi, Peristeria,
and Tragana

ROOM 2

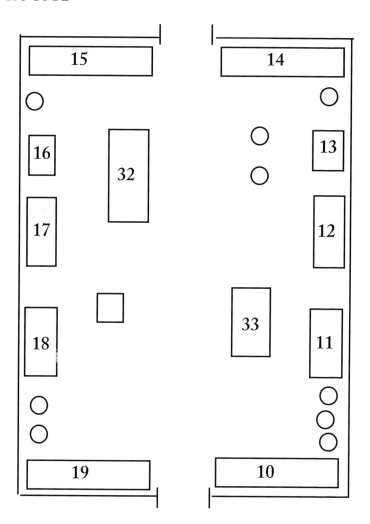

CASE 10   **Pottery from pantries**
Top: Drinking cups from pantry 20
Middle: Drinking cups from pantry 20
Bottom: Serving and drinking vessels
from pantry 20

CASE 11   **Frescoes**
Lion and griffin from queen's hall 46
Dogs, hunting scene fallen into bath-
room 43

CASE 12   Frescoes

Men with dogs and tripods, fallen into corridor 48

Head of stag found in pantry 19 [fallen?]

Flowers from washroom 53

White crocus from court 47

Seated women, nautilus frieze from inner propylon 2

Nautilus found in corridor 16 [fallen?]

Seated woman, fallen into oil magazine 23

Seated woman from outside to northwest

Architectural façade from court south of portico

CASE 13   Jars from storeroom 32

CASE 14   Pottery from pantry 60
Top: Cups
Middle: Jars, bowls, drinking cups, scoops
Bottom: Jars, bowls, cups, scoops, incense burners

CASE 15   Pottery from pantry 18
Top: Drinking cups
Middle: Jars, cups, dippers
Bottom: Bowls

CASE 16   Material from palace
Top: Pottery and bronze scraps from ramp 59
Middle: Stirrup jars and basin from court 47
Bottom: Pottery and other finds from propylon 1, propylon 2

CASE 17   Frescoes
Battle scene from hall 64
Rosettes from stairway 54
Lyre player from throne room 6

CASE 18   Frescoes found discarded on northwest and southwest slopes and under Wine Magazine
Heads and feet of male and female figures, nautilus frieze, bluebird frieze, bull leaper, offering table

CASE 19   Material from palace
Top: Pottery from pantry 20
Middle: Pottery from pantry 20
Bottom: Pottery from room 38, including strips of clay used to seal jars
Pottery and other finds from throne room 6 drinking cups from pantry 20

CASE 32   Finds from archives complex 7–8
Miniature kylikes, metal and stone finds
Two Venetian coins
Replicas of Linear B tablets

CASE 33   Finds from palace environs
Middle Helladic and Early Mycenaean potsherds from NW slope and under room 25
Byzantine potsherds from NE gateway
Middle Helladic, Early and Late Mycenaean pottery from south and southwest of palace and under room 65

OUTSIDE CASES
In front of CASE 13: Pottery from storeroom 32, bathroom 43
In front of CASE 18: Table of offerings from throne room 6
Other: Storage pottery fallen into room 38

ROOM 3

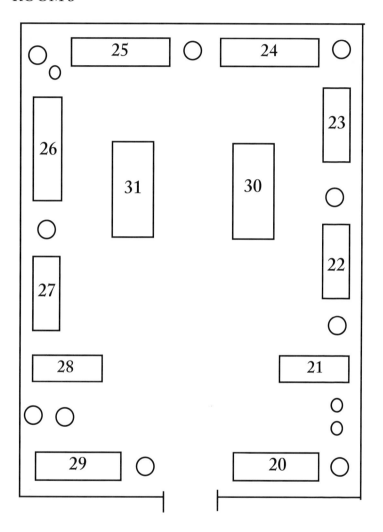

CASE 20 **Material from tombs at Pylos**
Top: Finds from Protogeometric
   Kokkevis tholos; Kokkevis chamber
   tomb
Middle: Finds from Tsakalis chamber
   tomb 8

Bottom: Finds from Kanakaris tholos 4;
   Tsakalis chamber tombs 4, 6, 9, 10

CASE 21 **Material from Pylos Lower
   Town and tomb**
Top: Drinking cups, mugs, and other

finds from Lower Town, southwest of acropolis

Middle: Pottery from Tsakalis chamber tomb 8

Bottom: Finds from Tsakalis chamber tomb 8

CASE 22 Material from palace and environs

Top: Cups and bowls from pantry 21

Middle: Cups and bowls from pantry 21

Bottom: Finds from dump inside south angle of acropolis, southwest slope

CASE 23 Material from palace and environs

Top: Pottery from room 98, NE building

Middle: Finds from corridor 95 and room 97, Northestern Building
Finds from northwest slope and Lower Town
Finds from shaft grave under workroom 97

Bottom: Finds from dump inside south angle of acropolis, southwest slope

CASE 24 Material from palace

Top: Pottery from pantry 68

Middle: Pottery from pantry 68

Bottom: Finds from workshop 55; brazier and other finds from pithos under room 55; finds from area 101, Wine Magazine 105

CASE 25 Pottery from pantry 67

Top: Tripod cookpots and other vessels

Middle: Tripod cookpots and other vessels

Bottom: Scoops and lids

CASE 26 Material from palace

Top: Drinking cups and other vessels from court 42, bathroom 43

Middle: Pottery, some of it burned gray, and other finds from corridor 52, queen's hall 46, drain below room 53

Bottom: Stirrup jars from room 53

CASE 27 Material from palace

Top: Miniature drinking cups and other vessels from doorway between pantries 18 and 20

Middle: Drinking cups from pantry 19

Bottom: Finds from entrance 12, storeroom 27, room 39

CASE 28 Pottery from pantries

Top: Dippers from pantry 22

Middle: Bowls and other finds from pantry 22

Bottom: Finds from pantry 23, including clay twists for making Linear B tablets

CASE 29 Material from Pylos tombs

Top: Finds from Kondou chamber tomb 1

Middle: Scales, daggers and other finds from Pylos: Vayenas tholos 5 ("Grave Circle")

Bottom: Swords and other finds from Pylos: Vayenas tholos 5 ("Grave Circle")

CASE 30 Finds from palace

CASE 31 Finds from palace environs

OUTSIDE CASES

Between CASES 20 and 21: Horns of consecration from Area 101

Beside CASE 29 and between CASES 28 and 29: Pottery from Vayenas tholos 5 ("Grave Circle")

Other: Pottery from various rooms in palace

SELECT BIBLIOGRAPHY

Blegen, Carl W., and M. Rawson. *The Palace of Nestor at Pylos in Western Messenia* I: *The Buildings and Their Contents.* Princeton: Princeton University Press, 1966.

Blegen, Carl W., M. Rawson, W. Taylour, and W. P. Donovan. *The Palace of Nestor at Pylos in Western Messenia* III: *Acropolis and Lower Town, Tholoi, Grave Circles and Chamber Tombs, Discoveries Outside the Citadel.* Princeton: Princeton University Press, 1973.

Chadwick, John. *The Mycenaean World.* Cambridge: Cambridge University Press, 1976.

Davis, Jack L., ed. *Sandy Pylos: An Archaeological History from Nestor to Navarino.* Austin: University of Texas Press, 1998.

Lang, Mabel L. *The Palace of Nestor at Pylos in Western Messenia* II: *The Frescoes.* Princeton: Princeton University Press, 1969.

Shelmerdine, Cynthia W., and Thomas G. Palaima, eds. *Pylos Comes Alive: Industry and Administration in a Mycenaean Palace: Papers of a Symposium Sponsored by the Archaeological Institute of America Regional Symposium Fund.* New York: Fordham University, 1984.

ENDNOTES

1. We are grateful to Phoebe Acheson, Tucker Blackburn, and Sharon Stocker for their help in preparing illustrations, to Kerri Cox for encouraging us to make this revision, and especially to Aaron Wolpert for undertaking the thankless task of assembling color equivalents of the black-and-white illustrations used in earlier editions. We also thank John Bennet for his generosity in sharing with us his knowledge of the Palace of Nestor and the Pylos area.

2. "Mycenaean" here refers to the Late Mycenaean period (Late Helladic IIIA–B, ca. 1400–1200 B.C.). The Palace of Nestor was constructed ca. 1300 B.C., at the beginning of Late Helladic IIIB (LH IIIB), and was destroyed about a century later.

3. These were the so-called Osmanaga Tholos tomb at Charatsari near Koryphasion and the first of the two tholos tombs excavated at Tragana (see below, note 22).

4. The Early Mycenaean period covers the earlier centuries of the Late Bronze Age, prior to the construction of the first Mycenaean palaces (Late Helladic I–II, ca. 1680–1400 B.C.). The Early Mycenaean "palace style" is named not after the Mycenaean palaces, which were constructed later, but after the palace of Knossos on Crete, where the style was current during the 15th century (1400s) B.C. The Middle Helladic period (ca. 2050–1680 B.C.) precedes the Late Bronze Age.

5. So many tholos tombs have since been found in Messenia that it is clear they cannot all have been for royalty, but were the preferred tomb type of the Mycenaean elite as well as royalty in this region.

6. Tiryns and Mycenae in the Argolid were excavated first in the late 19th century by Heinrich Schliemann: substantial remains of their Mycenaean palaces can be seen today. The Mycenaean palace at Thebes in central Greece is now covered by the modern city; isolated parts can be seen in various building lots.

7. The Linear B script is the system of writing used by the Mycenaean bureaucracy to record economic and administrative information. The language of the script (an early dialect of Greek) was deciphered in 1952 by a young British architect named Michael Ventris.

8. See bibliography.

9. There was also a Mycenaean predecessor to the extant Late Helladic IIIB palace.

10. This gateway lies just inside the fence that now surrounds the site, and is visible from the lower parking lot and the path to Tholos IV.

11. It is very likely that there was a doorway from the outer portico into room 7, as restored. Recent investigations below floor level strongly suggest that another doorway connected the inner portico with room 8.

12. Bath attendants are among the personnel mentioned in Linear B tablets from Pylos.

13. The name refers to the stirrup shape of the handle. These jars were containers for olive oil (Fig. 23).

14. The northeast entrance to the Main Building, subsequently blocked off by the addition of courts 42 and 47, is similarly at right angles to the axis of the throne room.

15. The tholos tomb (Tholos IV), outside the fence of the archaeological site, is reached from the lower parking lot northeast of the palace.

16. *The Palace of Nestor at Pylos in Western Messenia* III (see bibliography), pp. 134–176. The grave pits and the floor have been covered, and no remains are visible, but finds are on display in room 3 of the Chora Museum (see below).

17. Tholos III, commonly called the Kato Englianos Tholos, is located immediately north of the modern asphalt road, and is clearly signposted.

18. The chamber tombs are visible, but are difficult to locate and are not signposted.

19. This tomb has often been called the Osmanaga Tholos, Osmanaga being the former name of Koryphasion. From the intersection with the road to Romanou, drive northeast ca. 500 m toward Chora. Signposted. Turn right, following the earthen track right to its end. The tholos tomb lies a short distance farther to the southeast in an open field.

20. Drive ca. 7 km north of Pylos on the main road to Chora. Turn left on an earthen road to the village of Petrochori. Signposted. At the outskirts of Petrochori, a track leads south to Voidokoilia Bay after 1.5 km.

21. This settlement of Coryphasion should not be confused with the village of Koryphasion, which has assumed the ancient name in modern times.

22. These tombs are often called the Tragana tholos tombs, although they are more easily approached from Romanou than from the village of Tragana. At the edge of town, take the asphalt road to Tragana. Cross the bridge over the Selas River. Signposted. Turn left onto an earthen track. Signposted. After ca. 500 m (1,625 feet), a path leads to the right toward the tombs.

23. No remnants can be seen. The site lay on the outskirts of Tragana, along the earthen road to Ambelophyto.

24. Several of the chamber tombs can be easily visited. From the Archaeological Museum of Chora, follow the asphalt road toward Vlachopoulo. Signposted. After a short distance turn left onto an earthen road and park. There are tombs to both left and right of the road, as well as the foundations of a Roman bath.

25. Drive ca. 500 m from Chora in the direction of the Palace of Nestor. Turn left onto the asphalt road to Myrsinochori (ca. 3 km). At the outskirts of the village, follow an earthen road left to the church of Panayia Routsi. Signposted. The tholos tombs are located in the yard of a small house south of the church.

26. The site has been largely filled in since its excavation by the Minnesota Messenia Expedition, but a tholos tomb can still be visited. It lies on a high ridge immediately west of the crossroads of the Kalamata–Pylos and the Rizomylo–Koroni highways and can best be reached by asking directions in the village of Karpofora (signposted).

27. The town of Chora is 3 km north of the site along the main road. The museum is at the far end of town (signposted).